Contents

How have toys changed?

What kind of toys and games do you play with at home? Do you think children were playing with the same types of toys a hundred years ago?

Look at this picture from 1898. A toy that many children had in the past was a doll's house. However, children had fewer toys then. They often made their own toys and games, or used their imagination.

1898

WET

WET PAINT

Then and now

Why did many children in the past make their own toys and games? Do you and your friends make up your own games?

6

How have things changed?

Toys and Games

James Nixon

W

FRANKLIN WATTS

LONDON • SYDNEY

First published in 2008 by
Franklin Watts
338 Euston Road
London NW1 3BH

Franklin Watts Australia
Level 17/207 Kent Street
Sydney NSW 2000

ISBN: 978 0 7496 7840 1

Dewey classification number: 688.7'2

A CIP catalogue record for this book is available
from the British Library.

Planning and production by Discovery Books Limited
Editor: James Nixon
Designer: Rob Norridge

Photographs: p6 The Robert Opie Collection, p7 (top) The Robert Opie Collection, p7 (bottom) Bobby
Humphrey, p8 (top) V&A Images/Victoria and Albert Museum, p8 (middle) Ian Winton, p8 (bottom)
Bobby Humphrey, p9 Bobby Humphrey, p10 (top) Bobby Humphrey, p10 (middle) The Robert Opie
Collection, p10 (bottom) Bobby Humphrey, p11 Bobby Humphrey, p12 (top) Christie's Images Ltd.,
p12 (left) Bridgeman Art Library, p12 (middle, bottom) Beamish Museum, Photographic Archive,
p13 Bobby Humphrey, p14 Christie's Images Ltd., p15 (top) Bobby Humphrey, p15 (bottom) Rebecca
Hunter, p16 (top, left) Bobby Humphrey, p16 (middle) Beamish Museum, Photographic Archive,
p16 (bottom) Ian Winton, p17 (top, right) Bobby Humphrey, p17 (left) istockphoto.com, p18 (top) The
Robert Opie Collection, p18 (bottom) Mary Evans Picture Library, p19 Bobby Humphrey, p20 Topham
Picturepoint, p21 (top) istockphoto.com, p21 (bottom) Nicholas Rjabow/istockphoto.com, p22 The
Robert Opie Collection, p23 Bobby Humphrey, p24 (top) Bill Bridges/Getty Images, p24 (bottom) Tony
Boxall/Mary Evans Picture Library, p25 Bobby Humphrey, p26 Jeffrey W. Myers/Corbis, p27 (top) The
Advertising Archives, p27 (bottom) Bobby Humphrey..

Cover photos: (top) The Advertising Archives, (bottom) Bobby Humphrey.

Franklin Watts wishes to thank the following for their kind permission to use their material:
Disney/Pixar, Hasbro, Lego, MGA Entertainment, Nintendo, WowWee Toys and Character Toys.

Printed in China

Franklin Watts is a division of Hachette Children's Books, an Hachette Livre UK company.
www.hachettelivre.co.uk

Sometimes toys are handed down through the **generations**. Many old doll's houses are still in use today, like this one from **Victorian** times.

Find out for yourself

Ask your parents and grandparents what toys they played with. What differences are there between their toys and yours?

Now

Many of the toys produced now are similar to the toys that children played with in the past. Here is a modern doll's house. It is mostly made from plastic. Old doll's houses were made from wood.

Changing materials

One of the biggest differences between toys then and now is the materials that they are made from.

In Victorian times, a wealthy child might have owned a rocking horse. The horses were made from beautifully carved wood.

In the early part of the twentieth century, a lot of toys were made out of tin. This is a **clockwork** tin elephant.

These toy farm animals from the 1950s are made from a metal called lead. Lead is no longer used in toys because we know it is **poisonous**.

Then and now

Look at the farm animals then and now. Make a list of similarities and differences.

Since the 1940s, more and more toys have been made using man-made materials. Look at this modern rocking toy. It has a bear to sit on instead of a horse and it is made out of soft **synthetic** materials.

Then and now

Would the old or new rocking toy be more comfortable to sit on?

Woods and metals are still used in toys today, but plastic is more common. This **electronic** robot called Robosapien is mostly made from plastic.

What are the advantages of plastic? Why is it used so much today?

Many toys that were once made from metal are now produced in plastic, like this modern farm set.

Board games

Board games have been popular for a very long time.

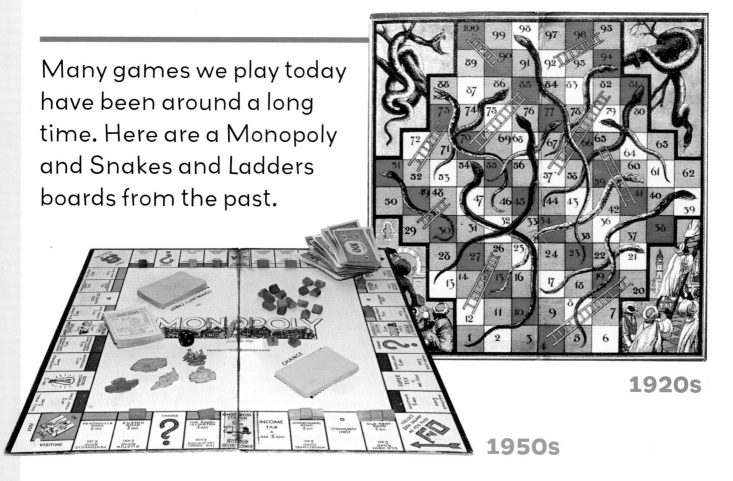

Thousands of years ago, the Egyptians were playing a board game called Senet. Pictured above is a modern **recreation** of the game. The winner is the first player to get their pieces home. Instead of a dice, Egyptians threw wooden sticks.

Many games we play today have been around a long time. Here are a Monopoly and Snakes and Ladders boards from the past.

1920s

1950s

Now look at the modern Snakes and Ladders and Monopoly. The rules of these games have not changed, but the board and pieces look different.

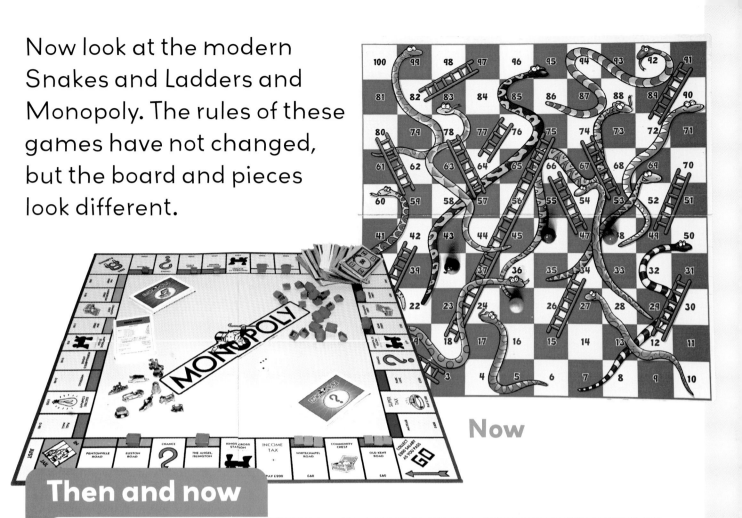

Now

Then and now

Compare these games to how they looked in the past. Which Snakes and Ladders board do you like best? What differences can you see between the two Monopoly sets?

Today, there is a wider choice of board games. Some games are based on luck. In other games, you have to show some sort of skill. Do you know what skill you need in the game of Operation?

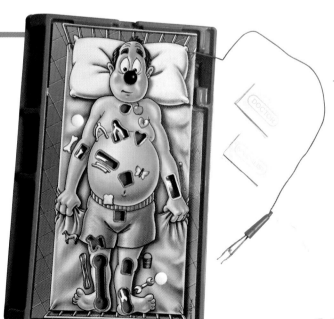

Dolls and action figures

Children have played with dolls for centuries. In Roman times, dolls were carved out of wood or stone, like this one.

In Victorian times, the dolls were usually made from **porcelain** or wax. Look at this wax doll. Wax dolls looked very **realistic**.

Porcelain dolls, like this one, were cheaper than wax dolls but they broke quite easily.

What do you think happened to a wax doll if it was left too close to the fire?

Parents in the past often made dolls out of cloth for their children. These were called rag dolls.

Since the 1950s, dolls have usually been made out of plastic. The first Barbie doll went on sale in 1959.

Today, Bratz dolls are very popular. They dress in fashionable clothes and come with **accessories** such as mobile phones and make-up.

Then and now

Do you think modern dolls are more fun to play with? Why?

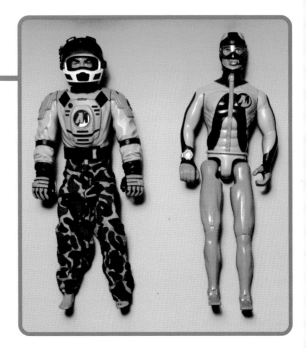

Many dolls now have moving body parts and some can talk. Modern dolls of soldiers or superheroes are especially popular among boys. This is Action Man. He comes in different outfits.

Soft toys

In 1902, a new toy was designed. It was named the teddy bear. Teddies quickly became best-sellers all over the world.

1910

Look at these teddy bears from 1910. The bears then looked like real bears. They had pointed **muzzles** and moving joints. The eyes on soft toys were made out of glass.

Today, teddy bears look less like real bears. They have flatter faces and no joints. The eyes are made out of plastic. This modern teddy bear can talk back to you when you press his paws.

Now

Then and now

The first teddies had quite hard bodies. The synthetic materials now used in bears and other soft toys make them a lot more soft and cuddly.

All sorts of soft toys can now be bought as well as bears. Many soft toys are characters from children's books, films and television programmes.

Children have always wanted to have models of the vehicles they see around them.

These model cars (right, below) are from the 1950s.

This tiny lorry was one of the first Matchbox cars. They were given that name because they could fit inside a matchbox.

In the past, clockwork vehicles were popular. You could wind up the toy with a key, let it go, and then watch it move. Here are a couple of wind-up toys from the 1940s.

Can you see where you put the handle in this car to wind it up?

Today, children still collect toy vehicles. Model cars can be pushed around on plastic road mats.

Moving toys are usually powered by electricity now. Batteries produce electricity. This battery-powered car (right) is being moved by a **remote control**.

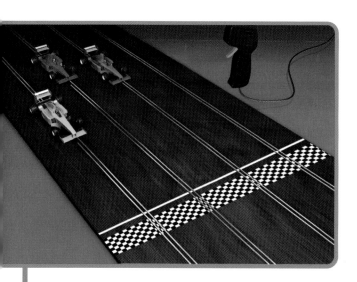

You can race cars against each other on a Scalextric track. The cars pick up an electric **current** that runs in the grooves of the track.

Then and now

Can you think of a reason why clockwork toys might be better than battery-powered toys?

Making things

In the past, girls and boys often played with different toys.

1930s

Construction kits were typically boys' toys. Girls may have had something like a needlework set or this wool-winding kit.

Wool Winding FOR WEE FOLKS

Dinner Card

Greeting Card

SPEAR'S GAMES

Can you work out what children did with this toy?

In the 1920s, Meccano became a popular toy with boys. Sheets of metal could be bolted together to make all sorts of things. The only tools you needed were a screwdriver and spanner.

MECCANO
Trade Mark Regd.

The Toy that grows with the Boy

Prices do not include transport or insurance.

M/CF/2 EXPORT STERLING 1956

1920s

A company from Denmark, called Lego, introduced a new type of construction kit in 1949. Buildings and other things, such as vehicles, could be made from plastic bricks that locked together.

In this modern set, three different vehicles can be made from the same pieces.

Now

Then and now

Do boys and girls still play with different toys today?

Lego is still very popular today, with boys and girls.

Outdoor games

Although children had fewer toys in the past they had just as much fun.

Children made up their own games and often played them in the street. Hopscotch, ball games and chasing games were popular.

Then and now

Compare the rollerskates in this picture to the modern ones on the opposite page.

1950s

Streets were safer 50 years ago as there was less traffic on the roads. The children in this photo are gliding along the pavement on rollerskates.

Many outdoor games have changed little in hundreds of years. Hopscotch, follow my leader and tag have always been favourites. Rollerskating is still popular today.

Then and now

Make a list of all the outdoor games that you like to play with your friends. Which ones would have been played a hundred years ago?

Now

There is more traffic nowadays. Children have to make sure they find somewhere safe to play. Special parks have been set up for children to play with modern toys like skateboards.

Puzzles

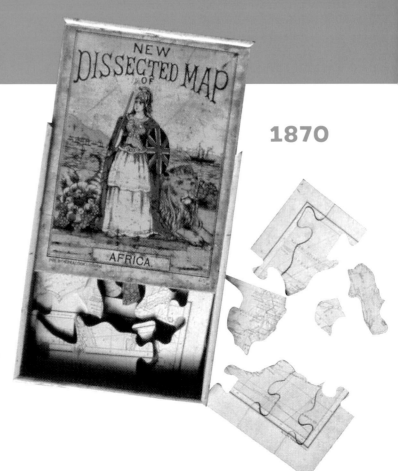

Many toys in the past were made to be educational as well as fun.

Early jigsaw puzzles were often pictures of maps to teach children geography. This puzzle (right) from 1870 is a map of Africa.

Then and now

Compare these puzzles to the modern ones. What differences are there in the shapes of the pieces? What differences are there in the way the pieces fit together?

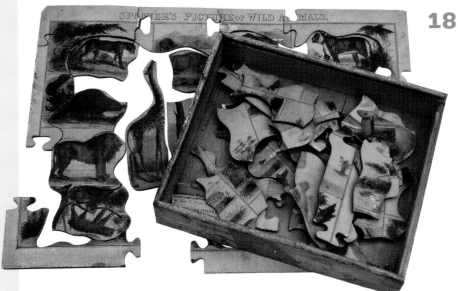

1870s

Over a hundred years ago, most jigsaws were made out of wood, like this one of wild animals. The pieces were cut into shape by hand.

Today, jigsaw puzzles are usually made out of thin cardboard. However, some jigsaws are still made from wood. Puzzles are often educational, too. These modern puzzles show maps of the British Isles and Europe.

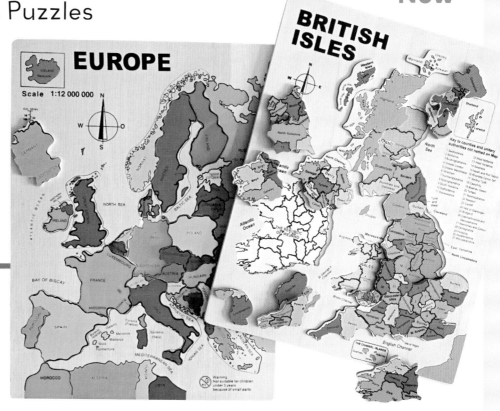

You can now find jigsaws of almost any picture. This cardboard puzzle is a picture from the animated film 'Cars'. Today, jigsaw pieces are cut into shape by a machine.

Crazes

Sometimes things are extremely popular but only for a short period of time. This is known as a craze.

There have been many toy crazes over the years. In 1957, a plastic hoop called the hula hoop was invented that you could swing around your waist.

1958

Quick sellers

Hula hoops went on sale in 1958 and 20 million were sold in the first six months.

1970s

In the early 1970s, the spacehopper was the toy every child wanted. It was an **inflatable** ball that you could bounce on.

Today, the latest craze might be a television series such as 'Doctor Who'. This show has been very popular with children and a lot of toys have been made that are linked to it.

Do you think crazes last long? Can you think of a craze that you took part in that has already ended? What is the new craze among your friends?

Toys based on the recent 'Transformers' film are popular as well. This Transformer's helmet changes the sound of your voice when you wear it.

Computer games

Victorian children would be amazed by the computer games you play today.

By the end of the 1980s, it was common for a child to have a games console. On these machines they could play different games on a television screen.

1988

The child played the game by using a controller called a joypad, or a joystick. The games then were very simple to play and they did not look very realistic.

Then and now

Do you think children in the past had as much fun playing computer games as you do?

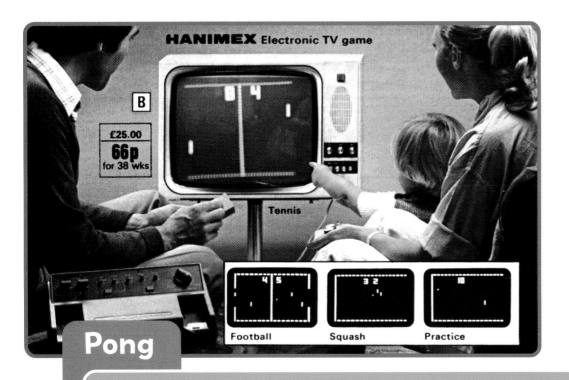

Pong

One of the very first computer games was a simple electronic tennis game. It was called Pong! Look at the picture. What other sports did Pong allow you to play?

Today, computer games look and feel a lot more realistic. Look at this modern tennis game on the Nintendo Wii.

Now

The children are controlling their characters on screen by swinging the controller as if it were a tennis racket. It is just like the real thing!

Glossary

Accessories Extra parts for something.

Clockwork Describes a toy that works when it is wound up with a key.

Construction Building or making something.

Current A flow of electricity through a wire.

Electronic Describes machines that are worked by small amounts of electricity.

Generations A generation is the period of time that it takes for children to grow up and have children of their own.

Inflatable Describes toys that need to be filled with air.

Muzzles A muzzle is the nose and mouth of an animal.

Poisonous Describes a substance that harms you if it gets into your body.

Porcelain Very fine china.

Realistic True to life.

Recreation Something that has been made to look like something from the past.

Remote control A system of controlling a machine from a distance using radio or electronic signals.

Synthetic Made from materials that are man-made, rather than natural.

Victorian Relating to the reign of Queen Victoria which lasted from 1837 to 1901.

Further information

Places to visit:

V&A Museum of Childhood, London (www.vam.ac.uk/moc/)
This museum houses one of the finest collections of childhood related objects in the world.

The House on the Hill Toy Museum, Essex (www.stanstedtoymuseum.com)
The large collection of toys in this museum ranges from the late Victorian era through to today.

Ilkley Toy Museum, West Yorkshire (www.ilkleytoymuseum.co.uk)
The many exhibits in this museum include dolls, doll's houses, teddy bears, tin toys, lead toys and games.

Websites:

www.museumeducation.bedford.gov.uk/bedfordbytes/toys/index.htm
has an activity where you can sort pictures of toys into old and new

http://tlfe.org.uk/clicker/flashhistoryks1/toys.swf
for a slideshow showing how toys are different from those in the past

www.ngfl-cymru.org.uk/vtc/how_toys_change/eng/Introduction/
introduces children to toys from the past with interactive activities, such as timeline building

Books to read:

At Play (A Victorian Childhood), Ruth Thomson, 2007 (Franklin Watts)
Toys and Games (Changes), Liz Gogerly, 2004 (Wayland)
Toys and Games (Everyday Inventions), Jane Bidder, 2006 (Franklin Watts)
Toys and Games (History Snapshots), Sarah Ridley, 2007 (Franklin Watts)
Toys and Games (Ways into History), Sally Hewitt, 2004 (Franklin Watts)

Index